A Bite-Sized Business Book

Write to Win
How to Produce Winning Proposals and RFP Responses

Ian Benn

Although the publisher and author have used reasonable care in preparing this book, the information it contains is distributed as is and without warranties of any kind. This book is not intended as legal, financial, social or technical advice and not all recommendations may be suitable for your situation. Professional advisors should be consulted as needed. Neither the publisher nor the author shall be liable for any costs, expenses or damages resulting from use of or reliance on the information contained in this book.

The right of Ian Benn to be identified as the author of this work has been asserted by him in accordance with the Copyright, Design and Patents Act 1988

© Ian Benn 2015
ISBN: 9781521061367

Bite-Sized Books Ltd Cleeve Croft, Cleeve Road, Goring RG8 9BJ UK
www.bite-sizedbooks.com
information@bite-sizedbooks.com
Registered in the UK. Company Registration No: 9395379

Bite-Sized Books Ltd
Cleeve Croft, Cleeve Road, Goring RG8 9BJ UK
information@bite-sizedbooks.com
Registered in the UK. Company Registration No: 9395379

Contents

Introduction

Chapter 1
The Gotchas – Common Mistakes and How to Avoid Them

Chapter 2
A Secret Blend of Herbs and Spices?

Chapter 3
What's the Story?

Chapter 4
The Killer Management Summary

Chapter 5
The Long List of Questions

Chapter 6
Pricing Strategy

Chapter 7
Management Summary

Bite-Sized Books

Introduction

The Request for Information has landed with a blood-quickening thud on your desk. The clock is ticking. The stakes are possibly even higher than you realise.

Writing a winning proposal can transform a company and the life and career of its author. Win a major deal and you establish a solid base for a whole new source of growth for your company and, as an employee, establish yourself beyond all doubt as someone who personally made the business more successful. A wise old head hunter once told me that, career progression depends on only two things: adding value to your employer; and being seen to add value to your employer. There are few faster, higher profile ways to bring value than being the architect of a winning bid.

Conversely, losing is painful and damaging, not least because of all the cost and effort that goes into the process. Even worse is to come second after a long, protracted process. All that effort, time and motivation wasted at the last moment. In fact there is an even worse outcome – winning a deal that is bad for the company. That might be because the pricing would have been too low to sustain a profit, but equally, it might be because the proposal was poorly worded and ambiguity in the words might have led to expectations that can never be met.

This brief book will help you to win great business, grow your company and transform your career. And all in around 40 pages.

Chapter 1

The gotchas – 14 common mistakes and how to avoid them

Where do proposals go wrong? There are 14 common problems, most of which fall into the category of "Never forget both why you are writing the document, and for whom":

1: Don't forget why you are writing the document

The goal is not to just respond before the deadline; the goal is to win the deal. Particularly when it is a long document with a short time to respond, people often lose focus on the end result, fixating instead about getting all the questions answered before the submission deadline. Often the bid leader chops the document into pieces and parcels each out to different experts within the business to answer their own specialist questions. As a result, every question is answered, but often in different styles, with lots of duplication and different assumptions as to what is covered in the other sections. The result? The document will be difficult to understand and there is unlikely to be a coherent theme in the final document.

Tackling a heavy set of questions is daunting and it is easy to focus on the weight of the task, but in fact there are two things you must achieve in order to win. The first is to answer every question in a positive and easily understood way; and the second is to tell a simple story about why you are the best choice for the prospect to make.

That means everyone involved needs to understand the whole picture and their role in answering their sections. It also means you need to allow time at the end to pull the document together into a coherent and persuasive form.

2: Make sure it is winnable

Submitting a quality proposal is an expensive, time-consuming and emotionally draining experience. There is no point in doing it if you cannot win. How can you tell?

- Does the RFP (Request for Proposal) document use language and terminology that is unique to one of your competitors? If so, the

chances are that they influenced the RFP to the point of ensuring that they are the only compliant bidder.
- Do you have a relationship with the prospect? If not, you are already at a disadvantage. This book is not about sales processes and techniques, but if you don't know the prospect, then you should assume that at least one of the other bidders does. If you really want to win, you are going to have to work hard to stand out and you may need to run a fast and high stakes sales campaign in order to ensure that you can stand out.

Would you buy you? Some time ago, I was involved in a bid to sell a complex software processing solution to a very large corporate. The value was huge, but they already had a provider who was doing a perfectly adequate job for them and, to my mind, the cost and risk of changing systems would probably have outweighed any benefits. Unusually, I was invited to meet their procurement team for an initial briefing session as a part of the process. At the end, we were given the chance to ask questions and I asked, "I don't understand why you would change from your current provider. If I were you, I would be looking at the cost and risk. Is this an exercise to renegotiate pricing with the incumbent, or is there something that they are letting you down on that is driving you to reconsider your approach?" This allowed us to make an informed decision as to whether to proceed and, if so, what to highlight in our messages back to the prospect.

3: Make sure you have enough time to do it properly

Have you got enough time to do a good job? If not, don't be afraid to ask for an extension, as long as you give a sensible reason. For example, something like, "We really want to have you as a client and we think we have a very strong fit to your needs. At such short notice, I do not want us to field the B Team. Would you be able to give us a few extra days so we can muster our most senior and experienced people? I want to make sure that the very people who will be responsible for delivering this service to you are a part of the bid process from the start.". In my experience, it is rare for a prospect to say no. Even if the prospect refuses, it won't hurt your reputation or chances of winning. In fact if they do say no, unless it is an unusually tightly controlled process, it can be a good indicator of their attitude to you as a potential provider. Perhaps you are only there to make up the numbers and they have really already chosen their preferred option. If that is the case, it is as well to know now before you sink all that time, money and effort into an unwinnable situation.

4: Look at it from the perspective of the poor, suffering people who have to read all these responses

Remember, selection is usually by a panel not an individual. Each has different interests and focus. Therefore make it easy to split the document up so that the finance, technical and executive teams can all clearly see the parts that they most care about.

Imagine being the recipient of a two-foot thick pile of densely typed technical responses. If there are a lot of bids, the first objective of anyone on the selection panel will inevitably be to try to whittle down the number of responses that they have to take seriously as quickly as possible. Therefore **the focus is usually on reasons to reject, not reasons to select** so therefore work hard to avoid answering "No" to any question. Nobody expects 100% compliance to a list of questions (in fact it can look suspicious), but a 90% fit is a reasonable goal. If you really can't meet the vast majority of the requirement, should you be bidding?

5: Tell your story in a succinct and compelling way

Nobody will thank you for making their selection job slower and more arduous than necessary. This is true throughout the document, but most especially in the management summary section where brevity and focus is the most important consideration.

Decision-makers tend to be busy people and avoid drowning in workloads by having exceptionally short attention spans. They will want to see a crisp summary with all the information they need in one place – including the pricing if it is part of the overall evaluation.

6: Don't make it hard for the reader to find information

Appendices should contain supporting information only. Don't send readers backwards and forwards to find the answer to a question. So, if the question is, "Does your software product run on an iPad, the answer should not be "See appendix 3, page 104."

As someone who has been on both ends of the tender process, I assure you that constant cross-referencing makes the reader seethe.

7: Be definitive

Check that you have answered every question with a "Yes", a "No" or a "Partial" before getting into details. However positive the content, a long, rambling answer always reads like a "No", but with a long excuse attached.

8: Cover yourself legally

Always have the phrase "Errors and Omissions Excepted" in the header of every page (you may abbreviate to E+OE). This mitigates the risk that you accidentally under-price or overpromise something due to a typing error or misunderstanding and that "promise" is later used against you in court after you have won the business. Of course this does not excuse sloppiness. And remember, for this approach to cover your risk you would need to demonstrate that the contentious phrase or section was truly an error.

9: Set a time limit

Always make clear that the proposal is only valid for a fixed time period. This will help you with future negotiations and will protect you where you are reliant on third party components which may go up in cost to you over time.

10: Don't go wobbly on pricing

Often proposal writers show a price and then add some words of equivocation. They will provide a clear, easy to understand matrix of fees and then at the end add something like, "The prices shown are open to negotiation." From the perspective of any competent buyer:

1. All prices are open to negotiation in any case
2. It sends a clear message that, either you think you have plenty of spare margin to give away or, worse, even you know that you are pushing your luck

As with any sales situation, you should simply state the deal and keep quiet until you get a response back from the client.

11: Get the formatting, the presentation and the grammar right

Sloppy writing or presentation is a powerful indicator of your company's attention to detail and therefore the quality of service a prospect might expect to receive from you. A reader may not know an adverb from a subjunctive clause, but everyone can tell whether something makes sense. Worse, poor grammar can lead to ambiguities which in turn drive mistaken expectations. These can lead to dissatisfaction, poor relationships and even legal disputes long after the bid was won.

On the subject of detail, it is a good idea to be consistent with your self-descriptor. If you are a company, it is considered best practice to refer to your company as a singular entity ie, "XYZ Corp is…", never "XYZ Corp are…". Partnerships are more commonly in the plural, "at XYZ LLP, we…". There is no golden rule here but consistency makes the document a lot easier to read so pick one and stick with it.

If you are not a grammar ace, I would recommend that you find someone whom you can trust to proof read the final document before it goes. Ideally they should be smart and well educated, but not too familiar with the detail. If you can't find someone appropriate, try reading the most important parts (such as the management summary) aloud. Does it sound like normal spoken English or do you sound like a dodgy lawyer? If the latter, you probably have too much flowery language in there.

A final thought on this point: I once received a CV from a prospective employee which started with a section on his unique personal qualities. The first strength he highlighted was, "Attention to detil". He didn't get an interview.

12: Try to understand the client's approach to the money

Ideally you will already be in some kind of dialogue with the prospect. If so, it is useful to understand how they intend to account for the project and how they want the costs to flow. Is a large capital expense, followed by a low operating cost better for them, or would they rather avoid capital expenditure and treat the whole thing as an ongoing operating cost? The pressures on departmental leads in large organisations change all the time, so you can never assume which would be best for them. As an example, in a technology company, capital expenditure is often very tightly controlled because a high capital spend can imply to the investor community (which often makes decisions based on very broad ratios), that the company is burning development costs on things that nobody wants to buy. At the same time every organisation faces pressure to meet quarterly or annual budgets and treating a cost as a capital expense can move costs out of the day to day profit and loss account and onto the balance sheet. That too can be attractive at different times in the annual cycle. Is a capital expenditure better or worse? It depends on the day you ask.

13: How much is too much?

I have been involved in many pricing strategy sessions where the sales lead has presented a proposed price for a service or product without understanding the impact on the prospect. Often they ignore the extra internal costs that the prospect will also face (quite often an order of magnitude more than the money they will spend with the external providers). Other times they might forget that the prospect is also going to need to buy other equipment or services. But the most common mistake comes when selling something to enable a commercial entity to bring a new product to market. The first question to ask there is, "Approximately how much money is their new business venture likely to make?" Sometimes this is difficult to guess, but especially if you are pricing based on usage volumes, it is worth trying. I have seen proposed pricing that comes to many times the total profit the client might be reasonably expected to make from the entire venture. That is very unlikely to work. I recently received a bid from a prospective supplier to outsource a part of my business for a price that was a little more than twice as much as it would cost me to do nothing and carry on as before. Unforgivably, in that instance, the supplier had access to all the data and would have been able to see that the numbers didn't add up if they had simply asked themselves the question, "In Ian's place, would I buy this?"

14: Jargons and clichés

Most people agree that jargon is annoying and to be avoided at all times. Unfortunately, people don't have a common view on what constitutes jargon and what is everyday language. In every company and every industry, we choose to rely on acronyms and jargon for speed of communication. When I joined my last employer, I was puzzled for ages about the constant reference to SMEs. We were a technology company selling to large banks and we didn't have anything to do with small and medium enterprises. It took me weeks to figure out that SME was nothing to do with small businesses and stood instead for Subject Matter Experts. The first rule of avoiding jargon is to notice when you are using it. If you have time, it is worth getting someone smart and educated, but from outside of your domain, to read through your document and see whether they understand it. If they do, you know you have a clear proposal. At the same time, explaining common terminology can come across as patronising. I think the best approach is to spell out an acronym the first time you use it but not subsequently. It is also worth considering a glossary at the back of the document in case you have missed anything. The good thing about a glossary is that once you have put it together, it is very light work to maintain it for future proposals and it can also form a useful on-boarding tool for when you hire new staff.

As to clichés, I will leave the final word in this section to William Safire: "Last but not least, avoid clichés like the plague; they're old hat".

The Gotcha checklist

Is my goal clear to me?	
Have I got enough time?	
Can I win?	
Am I thinking of the reader?	
Is the document brief and clear throughout?	
Is it easy to find information?	
Am I being definitive in my answers?	
Have I covered the legal side?	
Is the response timebound?	
Am I being clear and confident about pricing?	
Is the document well-presented and easily read?	
Do I understand the client's financial focus?	
Does the pricing make commercial sense for the recipient?	
Have I exorcised the jargon and clichés?	

Chapter 2

The Secret Blend of 11 Herbs and Spices*

Anyone can fry a chicken, yet few food companies have ever come close to the success of the late Colonel Sanders' Kentucky Fried Chicken, now KFC. Along with many others, most notably, Coca-Cola, competitive necessity forced them to keep their recipe secret; patents expire, whereas closely held secrets do not. Whilst keeping the secret to this day, Sanders did give one clue, saying that there was nothing in his mix that you would not find in your kitchen cupboard at home.

For KFC, then, their competitive edge has consistently come from their world famous "Secret blend of 11 herbs and spices" each on its own unremarkable. That, and serving food in a bucket, of course. What is your competitive edge?

Like the Colonel, you are unlikely to have any single ingredient that alone will mark your proposition out so the important thing is to lay out all the things that, taken together, enable you to offer you the best blend of product, price and service.

For each proposal, I tend to use a whiteboard or a big piece of paper rather than a PC for that stage. Ideally you want a good long list of strengths.

The next step is to disregard anything that is irrelevant to the prospect. There is no point in having great distribution in the UK if the client is only looking to expand into China.

For each relevant strength, think about the proof-points that can take it from a bland statement to a provable fact. That might be:

- Industry awards
- Certifications
- Quotes from customers
- Third party evidence of market share or company scale
- Audited figures (eg R&D spend, market leadership etc)
- The simple fact that nobody can argue – for example, you may just have the only product in your field with the relevant functionality

Objectively, looking at the list you have assembled, is it enough to persuade you that, in the client's position, you would choose yourself as the best possible provider? What about if you are a little more expensive than some others?

Once you are happy with the list, put them in priority order. If there are more than 7 or 8 things on the list, you may want to drop the last few on your list. Most people can only remember 5 or 6 things from any document or proposal so a very long list of benefits may be counterproductive, blurring the message and making you seem like just another company with an overenthusiastic sales pitch.

This is the raw material that will drive the messages in your management summary.

*With thanks to KFC Corp

Value checklist

	✓
Is this benefit relevant to the reader?	
Can I prove it?	
Have we got a reasonable number?	
Taken together does this make me unique or at least compelling?	
Would anybody else be able to make the same offer?	

Chapter 3

What's the story?

So by now, you have a clear view on the overarching message – your secret blend of herbs and spices. That will inform the answers that you provide throughout the document and it is important that you circulate that information to everyone involved in writing the content so that everyone understands the overarching message.

The way in which you turn that raw information into a response will depend on an understanding of the reader(s). Are they operating under tightly controlled rules? If so, you need to make sure that your format and structure meets that guidance. If you do not, you may be disqualified. In some cases, you are not even permitted to provide a summary of any kind. What then? I would advise that you still go through the exercise, but use a very cut down version of the output in a cover letter. That will get through the rules and the exercise will still help with the rest of the answers.

Reading styles

"There are two kinds of people in this world: Those who believe there are two kinds of people in this world and those who are smart enough to know better." – Tom Robins, Still Life with Woodpecker

Tom is probably right. There are a thousand theories about learning and communication style and it is easy to tie yourself in knots trying to accommodate every combination. Frankly, I wouldn't try, but it is worth thinking about a few easy ways to get through to different types. I tend to focus on three:

- Visual thinkers who best respond to pictures, charts and diagrams
- Data thinkers who are really only comfortable when they can see measurable data – financial models and statistics
- Conceptual thinkers who respond to a more emotional, descriptive form of communication.

In common with most people, I suspect am a mix of the three, but I like to think that, when buying, I tend to the middle one because it makes me feel as though I am taking a logical approach.

The best approach therefore, is to try to mix all three styles.

In order to cope with the sheer weight of all those fat responses thudding onto the desk, laden with hope and detail, the tender issuer will usually divide up the responses into sections and ship each off to relevant individuals to review and score. The technical or detail content may go to an IT, engineering or operations group, the pricing to procurement and/or the finance director and the summary to the business leads. Whilst it can be dangerous to generalise, pricing is usually analysed by financially focused individuals who may well consider any superfluous words as waffle, flim-flam and worst of all... "marketing". I'd therefore keep the pricing section especially uncluttered, concise and factual.

What if the cost part is a real strength? Where costs flow over a period of time (perhaps there is an up-front fee, with ongoing services and maintenance fees), , a graph can help clarify the offer even in the pricing section and help you to tell your story without being wordy.

Cultural sensitivities

This is always a difficult area not least because stereotyping is notoriously dangerous. Nonetheless, there are social norms to consider.

Take these two sentences:

1: "In order to assure performant and consistent service quality, XYZ Corp utilises ITIL standards to underpin its support process methodology"

2: "XYZ Corp keeps service quality consistently high by using the ITIL standard for service delivery"

Clearly they mean the same thing, but to my taste, substituting words like "utilise", for "use" and removing redundant, polysyllabic words makes the reading faster and easier.

It has been said that British business-people prefer simple language like the second example with short words. US executives are more likely to have attended business schools or extra-curricular MBA style courses and tend to be more comfortable with language that the Brits might think of as a little florid. Indeed overly simple language can be seen as a sign of intellectual weakness so think about varying the tone either side of the Atlantic.

For prospects where English is not their first language, long words are fine (most long English words come from the Norman invasion of Britain and therefore have a Latin root which makes them easy to understand for many other nationalities), but it is wise to avoid analogies, idioms and proverbs. Think what "raining cats and dogs" might mean to someone unfamiliar with that usage. English may be the most widely-spoken language, but expressions that we take for granted in one country can be confusing or misleading to others who expect the words to mean what they say. For the same reason, it is best to avoid uncommon words that will have them reaching for the dictionary. You should also assume that subtle messages will not get through and just stick with being direct.

Expectations on pricing will vary by country or region too. At one end of the spectrum, I have found that northern European clients tend to expect a fair, very clearly stated deal up front. If there is a sense that the bidder is holding back, it will quickly disqualify them from the process. In the Middle East and Africa, by contrast, there is an expectation that the pricing will be keen and clear, but that it is a starting point for what will be a very long negotiation. The negotiation starts with the opening offer in the proposal and ends sometime after hands have been shaken – if ever.

In some parts of the Middle East there is an expectation that after the whole deal is agreed, there will be a formal signing meeting between CEOs at which the client's boss will expect to be allowed to win "one last concession".

In the European and US public sector, where the bid process is often very controlled, there is little point in offering anything less than the best possible deal up front and the negotiation process will be clearly documented from the start.

These are useful considerations, but general observations, so if in doubt, ask: the worst that can happen is that the client refuses to tell you.

How do they speak?

Most organisations have a preferred writing style and you can pick up a lot from their web site, brochures or, in the case of public companies and charities, the chairman's statement at the start of the annual report.

Using the commercial language of profits and margins in not-for-profit sectors can be a source of friction. A bank will want to know that you are financially strong before they contract with you. Why? Partly because they want to know that you will be around to stand behind your promises but a cynic might say that it is so that, if something goes wrong later, they know that you are someone worth suing. By contrast, to many decision-makers in non-profit organisations, sections boasting about your growth and profitability are more likely to sow seeds of distrust. Their motives are different and you should invest the time to understand and reflect them. Charities almost always have a clearly stated and widely available mandate in the form of a charter. It is a good idea to read and reflect the language of that charter in your responses as it makes it easier for the reader to associate the benefits you are proposing to their own raison d'etre. Whether or not they are an official charity or another public body, remember to focus on what your service or product will do for the people the non-profit prospect exists to serve.

The bid team

For a large response it is common to rely on a wide team of experts including commercial and technical specialists from within your company and/or your partners. Often the RFI questions are shared out amongst the expert team without any briefing or expectation setting beyond a date by which the answers need to come back to the bid manager. This is a sure way to produce a response that is disjointed, contradictory and difficult to understand. If you are relying on a wide group, it is essential to kick things off with a formal bid team meeting or, failing that, a formally structured conference call.

The meeting should be chaired by the bid manager alongside, where appropriate, the salesperson that will get paid in the event that the deal is won. It can be a short session but it should be structured as follows:

- Introduction to the opportunity including what we know about the prospect, why we are bidding and broadly what we are selling
- The logistics – what do we need to do, by when and what happens next
- The secret blend of herbs and spices
- An overview of the technical solution if appropriate
- An open discussion about concerns and opportunities
- Question and answer session

A summary of actions – exactly who is expected to do what, by when; and public agreement from each participant that they are committed to meeting their deadlines

Either just before the bid kick-off session or, failing that, straight afterwards, every member of the bid team should receive a written follow-

up document that confirms:
- That they are a member of the bid team
- The sales messages (the secret blend)
- The technical overview
- The actions, owners and dates

For a critical or unusually complex bid, it is a good idea to schedule in an Executive Review Session at least a day before submission is due. This session is a short briefing for the senior stakeholders in your company to provide context. You can use the same content as the bid kick-off but at a slightly higher level – executives will be unlikely to be concerned at the technical detail, for example. Immediately afterwards, you should arrange scheduled diary time for each executive to read through as much of the document as they realistically can, after which you should recall the read-through team for comment, last minute changes etc. I would advise that, during the initial briefing, you make it clear that there is little time for changes so, unless something is easy to do or there is a true show-stopper, they should probably let it go.

What is the value of executive review if there is little opportunity for change? Three things:

1. It allows the senior staff to understand what the organisation is signing up to do
2. It is an opportunity for a brilliant last minute idea to surface from what should be the most experienced members of the organisation. Often these last-minute ideas drive the differentiators by which deals are won
3. It ensures that all of the accountable executives have bought into and implicitly approved the promises that you are making. That becomes much more important when you have won and are in the middle of delivering a difficult project.

Story checklist

	✓
Does the story reflect the proposition you developed in your "Secret blend of 11 herbs and spices"?	
Are we communicating clearly with visual, logical and data-driven thinkers?	

Have we used language appropriate to the nationality of the recipient?	
Does the pricing take into account the culture of the prospect?	
Are we using language appropriate to their sector?	
Have you built and briefed the bid team?	
Has the executive team bought into the offer?	

Chapter 4

Writing the perfect management summary

The perfect management summary has three sections:
1. The summary of benefits – the most important part
2. The commercial summary
3. The description of the service/products being offered and, if appropriate, the timescales

Summary of benefits

Unsurprisingly, the first part of the management summary should be a short section aimed at the most senior decision-makers; typically, the kind of people who read the summary of any document and then skip straight to the pricing page.

The summary is arguably the most important page or two of the entire document. It is therefore worth spending considerable effort on getting it right.

Coco Chanel, the fashion designer, famously said, "Less is more." Whilst I am told she was talking about the best way to design frocks, she could just as well have been talking about management summaries. Here are some simple rules:

- It is a summary so shouldn't contain any new facts that are not covered elsewhere
- If it is longer than 3 pages, it will not be read properly so be aggressive with the pruning shears
- For every sentence, ask yourself the question, will this help persuade someone to pick us. If not, cut it.
- Telling the prospect things they already know is unnecessary. Many management summaries have great tranches of text summarising the prospect's stated aims, often cut and paste from the RFI/RFP. This is a waste of valuable selling space and is incredibly boring for the reader.

- Equally, unsubstantiated or unprovable claims waste space and irritate the reader. Always be specific. The best test for a claim is this: would anyone else say the opposite? If not, then it is a statement of the obvious and therefore best avoided. For example, nobody would ever say:
    - We pride ourselves on our terrible service
    - Quality in absolutely nothing we do
    - Our customers always come stone last
    - We are proud to be a world follower
    - Our employees are our least valuable asset

There is no value, therefore in saying the opposite. Instead, make claims that you can back up with solid evidence. For example:
- Our clients tell us that they are delighted with the quality of service we provide. In the last 3 years, our client survey has generated a Net Promoter Score of +55. A copy of the summary is available if required.
- During the last 5 years, 8 of our clients have won prestigious service quality/innovation awards including…
- We recognise that your company is seeking to improve cost efficiencies as well as driving direct cost savings. Since our client, XXX implemented our product/service, they have seen a 35% reduction in operating costs. The full case study is attached in Appendix X for your information.
- Our focus on quality is evidenced by our ISO and BS certifications and the fact that our first time fix ratio is X%

Could other providers make similar claims? Possibly, but hopefully not all of them and taken together they tell a provable, action-focused story of a company that does a good job and can prove it

I think it is always good to be clear about why you want to win the business. There is always the obvious reason around additional revenue and profit, but I think it is good to talk about the desire for a new reference client, the glow of being a provider to such a prestigious customer or the drive to establish the company in a new and adjacent market. If you have done a good job and put a strong proposal together, the client may be wondering why you have been so generous and where the catch might be. This is the place where you put his or her mind at rest. "We have put very aggressive pricing together because we are keen to have an organisation as prestigious (innovative/respected/dynamic as appropriate) as a reference customer." Alternatively, if it is a public sector or philanthropic organisation, "We recognise the pride and motivation that serving your organisation will bring to our employees." Whilst not essential, I believe it is a good idea to show a positive motive for your company beyond the obvious direct profit contribution.

Add a little emotion into the mix. Different people make decisions in different ways and a winning proposal usually has to persuade several different people. Those who make fact-based, numerical decisions are usually well served throughout the response document. The management summary is where you can be a little more emotive. I think it is always good to state that you would be, "Proud to have the prospect as a customer and long-term partner". This is nice for the prospect to hear, is presumably true (or why are you bidding?) and helps to humanise what can be a very clinical process.

Structuring the summary of benefits

Structure is very important. It helps to avoid duplication and makes the summary quick and easy to read, digest and go back to. Below one I like to use. I have used capitals to mark the words for you to fill in and italics for the words that can be fairly standard in all summaries:

Introduction

"Thank-you for the opportunity to respond to this exciting new opportunity."

HERE'S WHY WE THINK YOU ARE A GREAT PROSPECT AND WE ARE A GOOD FIT, EXPRESSED IN A COUPLE OF SENTENCES

"In reviewing your requirements, MYCO believes that we have XX (BETWEEN 3 AND 6) unique strengths that can help PROSPECT NAME to fulfil its ambitions at the lowest possible risk and with the greatest future flexibility:"

Main body

ONE SECTION WITH A CLEAR HEADING FOR EACH OF THE 3-6

REASONS STATED ABOVE. START EACH SECTION WITH A COPY/PASTE OF THE BENEFIT STATEMENT AND THEN, BELOW EACH, SHOW AN EXPLANATION OF THE VALUE IF THAT IS NOT SELF-EVIDENT, A LITTLE MORE DETAIL ABOUT SPECIFCALLY WHAT YOU BRING AND, FINALLY, A LIST OF PROVEABLE, QUANTIFIABLE EVIDENCE AND/OR EXAMPLES.

Summary of that section

In short:

- HALF A DOZEN BULLET POINTS

"And finally: In putting this document together, we have endeavoured to meet your requirements technically and commercially based on our understanding of your needs. If we have been unclear, or a different approach is more appropriate, we would be very happy to engage in further discussions. MYCO would be proud to serve YOUR BUSINESS as a lasting partner."

Commercial summary

This goes directly below the summary of benefits. You may well have a more detailed pricing section elsewhere if required, but every exec will turn straight to the pricing whatever you do, so it is best to make it easy for them to find it. Note: in some rare cases, you will be instructed to provide pricing in a separate sealed section. Clearly in that case, you should not reference it in the management summary or anywhere else in the document as it will put you in direct breach of the rules of engagement.

The pricing should show the initial and ongoing costs in an understandable format that, where possible, matches the structure the client has asked for. Sometimes, that is either impossible, or there is a commercial reason to do things differently (this could be your big differentiator). For example, where the client is looking for an up-front fee, you may be suggesting a service fee based on usage, cutting their capital outlay and replacing it with a gentle ongoing operating cost. Clearly every situation is different, but I would advise that if you are taking such a radical approach, you let them know that you will be doing so, and ask their permission or advice first. However attractive your approach may be, if the procurement team are driving the process (or worse, an external procurement agency), it might get you disqualified before you get the chance to make your case so use this technique with care.

Where you can, try to identify capital costs separately from operating costs. This is important for decision makers in larger organisations where they may care more about the P&L impact than cashflow. Departmental decision-makers in large, cash rich corporates, for example, are typically measured on their in-year profitability. A large capital cost could be spread over 5 or even 10 years whereas an operating cost will hit them as they spend the money.

A lot of smaller companies assume that the accounting treatment is based on when the money is paid, but this is seldom the case. For example, consider a large corporate is spending $1m on technology and $500k on implementation. The technology bill is payable within 30 days of delivery, the services up to a year later. The corporate may choose to treat the whole project as a capital expense, written down over 10 years. In that case, they will pay the bill to you as due and add the $1.5m cost to their balance sheet. Every year, they will add $150k of cost to the business unit and reduce the capital value on the balance sheet by the same amount until, in ten years, it is down to zero. From the suppliers' perspective, there is no impact – you still get paid on time, but from the perspective of the budget-holder in the corporate, the in-year impact on his or her budget is just $150k. Asking questions about the budget process and treatment will impress upon the prospect the fact that you care about their business challenges and will help you put a winning proposal together.

Solution Overview

For more technical proposals, most responders provide a summary of benefits and then get straight into the detailed answers to questions without ever making clear exactly what their solution may look like. This can leave the buyer unsure exactly what you are proposing to do for them. Whether this is a service or a piece of technology, the client must be in no doubt what you plan to do for them and how it will feel to be a customer/user.

The solution overview is best structured with one or two diagrams and a short narrative to explain what the pictures mean. Of course you may have more comprehensive documentation in an appendix.

If you are dividing up a long list of questions and sections across multiple team-members, it is essential that they are given a copy of this section and that they read it carefully BEFORE THEY START. That way you are doing all you can to ensure that they are providing answers that are consistent with the overall picture. If their answers include their own pictures, you should try to ensure that they are complementary with the terminology and images that the overall solution uses. Often, different people, especially those from a technical background, have their own pictures that they like to use. Colours, descriptors, styles and even the overall vision can vary dramatically and that leads to confusion and uncertainty in the mind of the recipient. I would advise a draconian approach to the use of terminology and images.

Management Summary Checklist

	✓
Does the summary of benefits contain any new facts?	
Is it short enough (under 3 pages)?	
Is there a manageable number of reasons to select us?	
Have we provided proof for all of our claims?	
Is everything in the benefit summary relevant to the reader?	
Have we told them that we want their business – and why?	
Is the pricing completely clear?	
Is it shown in the way the prospect asked?	
Have you considered and made clear the cashflow and capital treatment options?	
Is there a clear solution overview?	
Do all the people in the bid team understand and buy into the overall solution description?	
Are all the diagrams and pictures consistent?	

Chapter 5

Answering the long list of questions

Questions in RFPs are usually written to have a straight yes/no answer. This is to make it easier for the people reviewing the responses to easily compare different bidders. Usually they weight the importance of each question (but don't tell you the weighting unless you get the chance to ask) and then simply add up the number of marks scored to get to a fairly crude score. A fit of more than 80% is usually good enough to be able to proceed to the next stage so don't panic if there are some gaps. In fact, if every answer is yes, it can even lead to doubts as to whether you are being honest in your responses.

So how do you structure the answers?

The worst possible answers you can give are either:

1. A long rambling answer which MAY be a yes, but is not definitive.
2. Any one word answer. If you say, "Yes", but don't say why or how, then it can look like you haven't really considered or understood the question. If you say, "No" without any explanation as to why, it seems like a: you don't do it and b: you don't care either.
3. Anything that is untrue.

Here's an example:

Q: can you provide 8 hour service coverage across the UK?

Terrible Answer: *We have 5 service centres, in London, Leeds, Bristol, Manchester and Glasgow delivering services to over 500 delighted clients and service over 1m consumers. We also provide service coverage in 18 other countries around the world.*

So is that a yes or a no? The writer thought he was saying yes, but the reader is not so sure. Most proposals contain loads of answers like this. They breed uncertainty, don't get you a tick in the box and can often make you come across as evasive and untrustworthy.

Better answer: *Yes*

At least this should get you a tick in the box. The problem is that a yes without an explanation cannot always be counted on. This is especially true if the question is complicated or unusually demanding. If the prospect thinks something is difficult to do and the answer is a simple yes, then they may wonder whether you truly understood the request or worse, you are choosing to say yes, without providing any context as to what degree or under what conditions. Are you hiding something?

Great answer: *Yes. We deliver an 8 hour response in every UK location which we ensure through our 5 service centres, which are situated in in London, Leeds, Bristol, Manchester and Glasgow. Should your business expand overseas in the future, we already have similar service coverage in 18 other countries around the world so we can grow with you.*

Here we get the question of yes or no out of the way up front. It's a simple Yes. Box ticked. All responses to such questions should start with a one word sentence; either "Yes", "Partial" or, if absolutely all else fails, "No". In every case, follow up with an explanation. Even what might at first glance be a no can be treated as a positive.

Let's try that service question again but this time, we will assume that we can only really give 8 hour coverage within an hours' drive of our service centres:

Q: can you provide 8 hour service coverage across the UK?

A: *Partial. We provide 8 hour service coverage in all major population centres – and typical response times are under 6 hours in London, Leeds Bristol, Manchester, Glasgow and Edinburgh. In more rural locations, response times can, on occasion, stretch beyond 8 hours. Experience, however, shows that over 90% of customers in your sector fall within the 4 hour response zone and, whilst we recognise that your organisation only requires 8 hour coverage, we find that resolution times that dramatically exceed expectations drive very strong levels of customer satisfaction, recommendation and repeat business. Indeed, our research shows that consumers who have had a problem that was quickly resolved tend to be more brand loyal than those who never had an issue in the first place.*

That said, if 100% coverage at 8 hours is essential, we are happy to discuss a special service arrangement but there may be a small additional cost for that which, given the high coverage already offered, has not been costed in at this point.

Note the structure here. We are giving a direct answer, explaining what we mean by the answer, justifying our position, protecting ourselves from being marked down (as best we can) and trying to outweigh any concerns with a stronger positive argument.

And finally if we can't honestly say even a partial yes, we must say a clear and straightforward no:

Q: can you provide 8 hour service coverage across the UK?

A: *No. We can and do provide 8 hour service coverage in all major population centres – and typical response times are under 6 hours in London, Leeds Bristol, Manchester, Glasgow and Edinburgh. In more rural locations, response times can, on occasion, stretch beyond 8 hours. Experience, however, shows that over 90% of customers in your sector fall within the 4 hour response zone and, whilst we recognise that your organisation only requires 8 hour coverage, we find that resolution times that dramatically exceed expectations drive very strong levels of customer satisfaction, recommendation and repeat business.*

Indeed, our research shows that consumers who have had a problem that was quickly resolved tend to be more brand loyal than those who never had an issue in the first place.

We recognise that you are operating in a tightly cost-constrained sector and In putting together our bid we endeavoured to focus on the best balance of service quality and low ongoing fees for you. By allowing the small risk of slightly longer service lead times for under 10% of the population, we have been able to build dramatic savings into the overall proposal.

So in summary, the only effective response options are:
- Yes. Explain
- Partial. Explain
- No. Explain how else we solve the problem or why we think there is a bigger picture to consider.

As with most situations in life, it takes a lot more words to say no than it does to say yes.

Questionnaire checklist

	✓
Have we given a straight yes/no/partial answer to every question?	
Have we shown that we understand the questions?	
Where we have had to say no/partial, have we given a convincing reason and/or an alternative approach to meeting the requirement?	
Where we have had to say no/partial, have we outweighed or minimised the objection?	
Do all the answers tally with the management summary and the solution diagram?	

Chapter 6

Pricing Strategy

There have been many books written about pricing strategy, almost all of which are far longer and more complex than this one. In this short section I will simply identify some principles and some factors to consider in building your response.

Firstly, I think it is always best to start by ignoring your costs and focusing on the price that you believe that will win the deal. Why?

1. It forces you to think about value to the client rather than your own internal factors
2. If you do it this way around you will find out quickly whether you can afford to bid, potentially saving a lot of time, money and heartache. If you start with the internal costs, you will find it too easy to kid yourself that the client will be happy to pay more than your costs and you could waste a great deal of time on an unwinnable deal.

So how do you decide the value to the client?

To keep things simple, let's assume there are two possible, non-overlapping drivers for buying something new:

1. To save money on current costs
2. To do something brand new

Naturally, most requirements are a lot more complex, let's keep things simple for now.

Cost savings – quick analysis

For cost savings, you need to use every route to help figure out current costs. This may come from inside knowledge, the client simply telling you, or an educated guess based on an understanding of how they currently do things. More often than not, you will rely on a combination of all three.

Here's an example based on a situation I have seen in a number of organisations over the length of my working life. We know that a client has been spending around $2m per year on running an old computer system. We also know that we could provide a new system for $2m that would then reduce that running cost by half. Over six years, at first glance, it seems like a simple decision:

	Year 0	Year 1	Year 2	Year 3	Year 4	Year 5	Total
Old System	2m	2m	2m	2m	2m	2m	12m
New system	2m	1m	1m	1m	1m	1m	7m
Saving to client	(2m)	1m	1m	1m	1m	1m	$3m

Year 0 is the period during which the new system is being built, but not yet operational. In that first year, the client has to continue to run the old system and, in addition, cover the implementation costs for the new one.

That said, even allowing for the cost of funds, a $3m or 30% saving sounds attractive. But these are not the full costs. When the system goes in, they are unlikely to be willing to switch off the old one without a period of, say, 6 months (50% of $2m) of parallel running just to be confident that they are secure. Now the figures are a little less attractive:

	Y 0	Y 1	Y 2	Y 3	Y 4	Y 5	Total
Old System	2m	2m	2m	2m	2m	2m	10m
New system	2m	1m	1m	1m	1m	1m	7m
Parallel run	0m	1m	0m	0m	0m	0m	1m
Saving to client	(2m)	0m	1m	1m	1m	1m	$2m

But that doesn't take into account the client's internal project costs. They may have a team of 10 people assigned to this project. With a fully loaded cost of let's say $100k each, that's another $1m up front.

They might also need additional hardware and software licenses (databases, middleware etc) for the parallel run and that could easily be another $500k during year 1.

Finally, no business case gets approval without a reasonable slug of contingency in the plan – 30-35% is pretty standard in the IT industry. For simplicity let's use 33%.

Now the case looks very different:

	Y 0	Y 1	Y 2	Y 3	Y 4	Y 5	Total
Old System	2m	2m	2m	2m	2m	2m	10m
Parallel run	0m	1m	0m	0m	0m	0m	1m
Kit for the parallel run	0m	.5m	0m	0m	0m	0m	.5m
Staffing costs	1m	0m	0m	0m	0m	0m	1m
New system	2m	1m	1m	1m	1m	1m	7m
Contingency	1m	.5m	0m	0m	0m	0m	1.5m
Saving to client	(4m)	(1m)	1m	1m	1m	1m	($1m)

Even ignoring the cost of funds, the client is $1m worse off over 6 years than if he or she does nothing. It might be possible to make this work if we could bring our up-front sales price and the annual running fee down by around half, but that may not be feasible and there is little point in winning a deal that loses money. The smart thing here is to have an open discussion with the client to validate the assumptions. If they say that we are not far off, then we know that this is not a programme that will work for either party and the best option is clearly to qualify out.

New opportunity – quick analysis

For something new, it is all about understanding enough about the prospect's business to try to work out the value that the new capability will bring them.

For example, a company may be looking to launch a new product. You know from their annual report that they are going to want to sell somewhere between one and three million of them over 5 years at an average retail cost of $30. You figure out that the price out of the factory gate is probably $15 and their margin is likely to be around 30% or $5. So you know that the total five year value to the client is $5-15m for which they will spend $10-30m. By making assumptions about the biggest costs (for example, share of fixed cost, raw materials, additional staffing, sales commissions and any other costs relevant to their particular sector) you should be able to get a broad view on what is left over for your part of the deal. That is not going to tell you your target selling price, but it will give you a sanity check on your assumptions. Let's, for example, imagine that you are selling a piece of manufacturing equipment with an up-front cost and well understood ongoing costs (power consumption, maintenance fees, spares, operators and any specialist fees). If you are planning to charge $5m up front and you know it will cost $2m per year to run (including power draw), then you have a total cost of $15m. That's probably a bit high for the above scenario. Can you afford to sell for less?

In the absence of detailed data, I think it is always better to use broad assumptions than to simply not try.

Cost up modelling

Having established a rough assumption of value to the client, you need to understand your true costs. This varies in difficulty hugely between industries. These are some considerations:

- Raw materials cost
- Share of fixed costs
- Additional staffing and overtime
- Contingency (unless the entire project will run at the client's risk)
- Third party components
- Maintenance costs on any third party components
- Costs to maintain compliance
- Recruitment costs (and staff churn costs)
- Staffing shrinkage costs (sick days, unplanned absence, training days and public holidays)
- Transportation costs
- Ongoing operational costs
- Inflation (for longer engagements)

Plotting the middle course

By now, you have two sets of numbers: a rough estimate of the value to the client, and a solid understanding of your own costs. Ideally this reveals a sensible margin that is in line with the market norms. These vary hugely by industry and you will have a solid view on your own business.

If, by selling at your assessment of the value to the client, the margin is too small to be acceptable, then, having checked your calculations closely, the best option is to go back to the prospect and share the problem and seek guidance or verification of your assumptions. They may well say no, but they may be sufficiently keen to keep you in the process that they will be willing to at least validate your thinking about their business. One again, there is seldom any point in selling below cost so this may be the time to walk away.

What if the margin is far higher than you would normally expect to make? In a tender situation, it is highly likely that you will be competing with other players in your sector. If not, why would the prospect go to the effort and expense of running a formal process?

So now you have to decide what your competition will do. If you believe there is a compelling business case for the prospect to buy at $5m and you have a cost of $500k, you need to decide whether the competition will bid at a 95% margin, or something less ambitious. That, of course, assumes that the competition has the same cost base as you. It may be that you are already providing a similar product or service to existing clients and your incremental cost for the new opportunity is very low as compared with people bidding for the first time. That, however, is unusual in most sectors.

Choosing your bid price therefore needs to take into account:

- Estimated value to the client
- Your knowledge of the competitors' behaviour
- Whether this is the best and final offer, or there are more rounds to be completed
- Your costs

There is always scope for subjectivity in the first three points, NEVER in the fourth. Over the years, I have seen many instances where bid teams kid themselves that their costs are going to be lower than they know in their hearts is reasonable. It is perfectly sensible to make a business decision to bid for something at an exceptionally low margin. It is not sensible to pretend that through some as yet undefined miracle, the margins will all work out OK in the end.

What to include

This can be a tricky area. I have spent most of my working life in hardware and software companies. In responding to a complex RFI, I have often had to rely on teams of technical experts to answer the detailed questions. Whilst it is a mistake to generalise, a lot of good technical staff are very focused on practical detail and think about things from the perspective of how they would run the project if they were at the client. That attitude makes them knowledgeable, empathetic and a huge asset to your team, but... It also means that they answer a lot of questions that have not actually been asked. I often see answers where the expert has included time, effort and cost for things that the client has not requested. That may be extra support for testing, or some extra tools and products that are not explicitly asked for, but without which the expert believes the project would be impossible to accomplish.

What's the harm? Well it depends on the behaviour of the competition. If 20% of the cost of your bid includes stuff that has not been specifically requested but that your experts "know will be needed," then you are unlikely to be price competitive. Worse, the client will never even know that you have included these elements whereas the other guy has not. Losing out to a less scrupulous competitor is infuriating, especially when you know full well that, in the end, the prospect will end up spending more with the other guy.

Some people choose to keep quiet about things that have been missed by the buyer – after all we are pricing what they asked for, not what we think they are going to need and, anyway, they might have a better way of addressing that gap that we hadn't considered.

Personally, I think you have to be clear with the prospect what you are proposing to do for them. Aside from the moral dimension (for me the primary consideration), nasty surprises later in the process are going to make delivery of this new project a nightmare for everyone and from a purely practical perspective, bad tempered engagements cost everyone more in the end.

I would therefore EXCLUDE the additional cost from the proposal, but make clear in the answer that, in "our professional opinion", we think they should budget for whatever the missing parts are, *whichever partner they select*. That way, you have been honest, kept your pricing competitive and been seen to add real value to their thinking in a way that, hopefully. your competition has not.

Pricing checklist

Item	✓
What is driving the requirement? Cost savings or new revenue?	
Do we understand their current costs?	
Have we thought about the client's other costs if they select us?	

How much How much money will the new initiative make the prospect over the relevant period of time?	
Is it enough to cover the costs of choosing us and still make an attractive return?	
Have we considered all our own costs and been honest with ourselves?	
Have we applied a sensible contingency fund?	
How do we think the competition will behave?	
Are our costs and those of the competition similar?	
Have we included anything the prospect did not specifically ask for?	

Chapter 7

Management summary

Thank you for investing the time and money to read this book. If you are about to start work on an important proposal, then I wish you every success and hope that you win. Moreover, I hope it will become the first in a whole series of significant positive steps for you and your business.

I believe there are 3 reasons why this book is the best thing you can read to help you win the deal:

1: Brief and focused

Many business books cover a broad range of subjects and run to hundreds of dense pages whereas this one is just under 10,000 words; just 50 minutes of content for the average English language reader.

2: Aligned with the task in hand

The book is structured to align with each of the sections you will need to complete and with a quick checklist for each chapter to help ensure that you haven't missed anything. Up front is a useful "Gotcha's" section to help you spot and avoid common mistakes.

3: A pragmatic approach to commercial issues

Books on pricing strategies often descend into complex and arcane theory. In this one I have focused only on the major considerations and provided enough tools to allow you to structure your own knowledge and thinking.

In putting this book together, I set out specifically to equip you to win bids. When you are successful, I would be very proud to think that this book played at least some small part in that achievement. If so, I would be forever very grateful for some positive feedback on the Amazon website.

Good luck.

Now *that* is a management summary!

The most successful people all share an ability to focus on what really matters, keeping things understandable and simple. MBAs, metrics and methodologies have their place, but when we are faced with a new business challenge most of us need quick guidance on what matters most, from people who have been there before and who can show us where to start. As Stephen Covey famously said, "The main thing is to keep the main thing, the main thing".

But what exactly is the main thing?

We created Bite-Sized books to help answer precisely that question crisply and quickly, working with writers who are experienced, successful and, of course, engaging to read.

The brief? Distil the *main things* into a book that can be read by an intelligent non-expert comfortably in around 60 minutes. Make sure the book provides the reader with specific tools, ideas and plenty of examples drawn from real life and business. Be a virtual mentor.

Bite-Sized Books don't cover every eventuality, but they are written from the heart by successful people who are happy to share their experience with you and give you the benefit of their success.

Made in the USA
Monee, IL
04 January 2024

51145004R00022